The Mistress was described as being "very Devilish." Three Slaves, finding it being difficult for 3 Slaves to support a family of 8 (whites) they had come to the conclusion to escape, to save themselves from being sold, had been threatened.

Left Parents; 1 Sister Mary Ann Williams, she wants to come away Henry left a wife, Harriet Ann - (Sophia Brown she is to be known by now) - He belonged to Eliza A. Brodins He is Smart, 22 yr's of age, Chesnut Color, &c. Two little sons, he was obliged to leave behind.

Cambridge

WILLIAM STILL
and His
FREEDOM STORIES

The Father of the
Underground Railroad

To Mom, who always inspires
—D. T.

Ω

Published by
PEACHTREE PUBLISHING COMPANY INC.
1700 Chattahoochee Avenue
Atlanta, Georgia 30318-2112
www.peachtree-online.com

Text and illustrations © 2020 by Don Tate

Edited by Kathy Landwehr
Design and composition by Don Tate and Adela Pons
The illustrations were rendered digitally.

On the front endpapers: pages from William Still's Journal C. Photographed at the Historical Society of Pennsylvania. Historians believe that the line running vertically through each page indicates that Still had transferred this information to the book he published, *The Underground Rail Road. A Record of Facts, Authentic Narratives, Letters, & C., Narrating the Hardships, Hairbreadth Escapes and Death Struggles of the Slaves in Their Efforts for Freedom*, which was based on his journals.
On the back endpapers: transcription of the text from the journal pages on front endpapers

Printed in March 2020 by Toppan Leefung Printing Limited in China
10 9 8 7 6 5 4 3 2 1
First Edition
ISBN 978-1-56145-935-3

Cataloging-in-Publication Data is available from the Library of Congress.

ACKNOWLEDGMENTS

First, thank you to my mom, Sharon Tate, who gifted me a copy of *The Biographical Dictionary of Black Americans* that she purchased at a garage sale, figuring that I might be inspired to write a book about one of the figures highlighted inside. She was right. Thanks to my editor, Kathy Landwehr, for her trust in me as a writer and illustrator, and for being a friend and supporter. Thank you to book designer Adela Pons, for her keen design sense and eye for detail. I am tremendously grateful to the following people who in some way played a role in helping me to tell William Still's story: Aslaku Berhanu, Librarian at the Charles L. Blockson Afro-American Collection, Temple University Libraries; Christopher A. Brown, Special Collections Curator for the Children's Literature Research Collection at the Free Library of Philadelphia; Samuel C. Still III (William Still family historian, third great-grandson of Levin and Sidney, also known as Charity, Still), chairman of the Dr. James Still Historic Office Site and Educational Center); the docents at the Johnson House Historic Site in Philadelphia; the Historical Society of Pennsylvania; and author-illustrator Jaime Temairik. Most of all, thank you to William Still for his important work.

WILLIAM STILL
and His
FREEDOM STORIES

The Father of the
Underground Railroad

Written and illustrated by

Don Tate

PEACHTREE
ATLANTA

This story begins
at a time when the United States
was split in two.

In the North,
Black people were free.
In the South,
they were enslaved by whites.

Slavery was a nightmare–
Backbreaking work under the scorching sun.
Threats of lashing–or worse.
No pay.

Children were separated
from their mommas and poppas,
brothers and sisters.
Sold away at auction,
never to be seen again.

Sometime during the 1700s,
Levin and Sidney Steel were held captive
on a Maryland farm, forced to work.
Their four children were too.
The family yearned to live free.

"I will die before I submit to the yoke,"
Levin told the man who enslaved him.

The two came to an agreement:
Levin was allowed
to work over-hours,
actually receiving a small income.
With the money he earned,
Levin purchased his freedom.

But freedom wasn't always fair—
especially to Black people.
Could a free Black man
remain in the South? Levin must have wondered.
Might he be enslaved again?

No chancing that.
Levin bid his family goodbye,
with a plan to return to rescue them later.
In a blink, he bolted North.

Sidney wasn't so fortunate.
There was no opportunity
for her or the children to purchase their freedom.

They remained behind, still enslaved.
A separation Sidney could not endure.

Torn and tormented,
she whispered a parting prayer for her two boys,
who were big and strong enough to fend for themselves.
Then she escaped with her two girls.

Sidney reunited with her husband
in the pine woods near Washington Township, New Jersey.
Now they were together—free as the wind.
They changed their last name from Steel to Still
to throw slave catchers off.

Their new life was good,
but living ached like an open sore.
Levin and Sidney longed for
the two sons they had left behind.

Over the years, the family grew.
Now there were fifteen children—fifteen mouths to feed!

Oh, how they struggled.
Money was tight. Food was scarce.
Shoes—if any—were hand-me-down.

In 1821,
the youngest child was born.
Sunlit eyes. Mahogany skin.
They named him William.
He grew quick as a weed.

Eight years later,
a neighbor was attacked late one night.
The man had once been enslaved
in the South.
He'd escaped and found peace in the pines.

Slave catchers tracked the man down.
They rushed at him. Cuffed his arms.
Beat him badly.

Thankfully, the man escaped again.
But he needed help—and soon!
The greedy men were still
on the prowl.

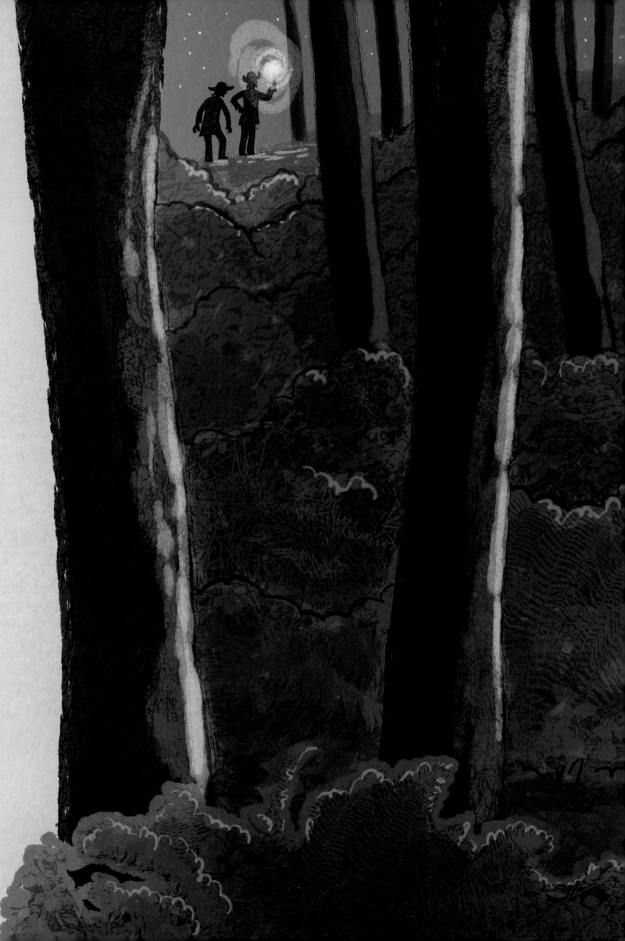

The neighbors called on William.
The young boy knew every nook and cranny
of the woods.

William led the man to safety,
some twenty miles away.
The experience defined the rest of his life.

William's father ruled the roost.

His rules: Chores were the priority. Education was not.

Schooling had to wait for rainy days,

when the ground was too soggy for work.

William looked forward to sharpening his mind.

But attending class

was no easy walk in the woods.

The North might have been free.

But free was not always fair—

especially to Black people.

One day
on the walk home after school,
white kids pushed William over the side of a bridge.
They laughed.
William plunged into the water.

Eventually, William's father
pulled him out of school.

Learning to read
would have to wait a few seasons.

Three winters later, conditions had improved.
William returned to class when he was seventeen.

He was there by sunrise,
home after dusk.

He studied spelling. Defined words.
Practiced enunciation. Learned math.
Before long,
he knew how to write too.

One wintry evening, warmed by a fire,
William grasped his favorite newspaper—
The Colored American.
An anti-slavery newspaper,
it was owned and published by Black people.

They published stories
that protested discrimination against Black people
in the North.
They printed stories
that encouraged emancipation of slaves
in the South.

The newspaper made William
recall his parents' stories.
Stories about slavery. Stories about escape.
Stories about his older brothers,
left behind to suffer in bondage.

William shouldered those stories
into the next chapter of his life.

By age twenty-three,
William craved more excitement,
as any young man would.
Life in the pines moved at a snail's pace.
Might the big city
bring bigger opportunities?

In 1844, he decided to find out.
With three dollars in his pocket, and a billion dollars in pride,
William planted himself north of the Delaware River
in east Philadelphia.

First things first:
he needed a job, and a roof over his head.
Neither came readily.

For three long years,
William bounced
from low-paying job,
to low-paying job.

He threshed clamshells.
Hauled wood. Laid bricks.
He peddled oysters.
Dug wells. Hawked clothes.
He worked on a dock, then at a hotel.
Barely earning the smell of money.

Long, cold winters. Grumbling belly.
No decent place to lay his head.
Not as glamorous
as the life he had imagined.

But then a new opportunity arose.
The Pennsylvania Anti-Slavery Society
needed an office clerk.
The pay was disappointingly low.

But the job might lead William
straight to the most prominent
anti-slavery organizers in the area.
With a foot in the door,
maybe he could help enslaved people
escape from the South.

Reluctantly, he accepted the job.
"I go for liberty and improvement,"
William wrote in a letter to his new employers.

In his new job, William sorted mail.
Emptied trash.
Swept office floors until his arms ached.
Not quite what he had hoped.

William's employers were doing
the work he hoped to do.
They were abolitionists
who spoke loudly against slavery.
They sponsored meetings. Signed petitions.
Published newspapers.

William worked hard, beyond his office duties.
He earned his employers' trust.
Gained their respect, their loyalty.
He climbed higher and higher,
until one day, he became the manager.

At that time, freedom-seeking people
were drawn to Philadelphia like a magnet.
It was the nearest free city to the slave-holding South.

They arrived daily by the dozens,
passengers on a secret network called
the Underground Railroad.

Freedom-seeking men and women,
young and old and in-between.
Running. Hiding. Praying.

They traveled from house to church.
River to swamp. Stop to stop to stop.
It was a dangerous, top-secret journey
from slavery to freedom.

The passengers who arrived in Philadelphia
were tired. They were sick and hungry.
Cut-up. Broken. Marred and maimed.
Frantic. Fearful. And fed up.
But hopeful.

William sought these travelers out,
and welcomed them into his home—
which was now a "station"
on the Underground Railroad.

One evening an unexpected passenger
arrived at his office.

The man was middle-aged.
Stooped back. Furrowed brow.
Threadbare clothes.
His name was Peter.
He was looking for his mother, his family.

Peter recounted his story.
William listened in awe.
Turned out, Peter had been enslaved
in the South
for more than forty years!
He'd gotten away.
Now he wanted to find his family,
who had escaped before him.

Peter recalled the names of his parents—
"Levin and Sidney."
He named one of his brothers—
"Levin."

William was thunderstruck.
Could this man be...his Peter?
His long-lost but never forgotten
older brother?

Yes, he was.

But Peter was confused
by William's news.
Was this some kind of trick,
to capture
and return him to the South?
He needed some convincing...

...from a mother who looked just like him.

Peter's story was sad. Tragic.
Miraculous.
And extraordinary.
And Peter's story restored his family.

Could other people's stories
reunite other families
torn apart by slavery?

From that point forward, William recorded every detail
about each freedom seeker
who passed through his home or office.

He recorded their names. Ages.
Boy or girl? Man or woman?
The hue of their skin—
Copper. Chestnut. Dark brown.

five feet seven inches

about 35

attempts to gain his freedom

John Jones & his wife

high; dark copper color

years of age

attempts to gain his freedom by flight

about 21 or 22 years of age

weighs about 150 or 160 pounds

Arrived__James Gibbs

of dark complexion and of slender

with her children

Who had enslaved them?
Where did they come from?
Where were they going?

It wasn't his job to do so,
but William thought these written records might help someday.
William's hard work didn't go unnoticed.
He climbed higher and higher
at the Anti-Slavery Society,
becoming the leader of a committee
assigned to help freedom-seeking people.
William corresponded
with other agents on the Underground Railroad.
He conducted interviews.
Counted money.
He planned the rescues of freedom-seeking people.
But his work didn't stop there.

William also recorded the stories
of people seeking freedom
on his line of the Underground Railroad.
In many ways, this was his most important work.

William and Ellen Craft,
a married couple,
escaped slavery in Georgia,
traveling on first-class trains.
They stayed in the best hotels,
and dined with a steamboat captain,
all in disguise.
Fair-skinned Ellen passed as a white man.
Her husband
pretended to be her slave.

A man enslaved in Virginia
climbed into a wooden crate
and had himself shipped
twenty-eight hours to freedom,
earning the name Henry "Box" Brown.

And on several nights,
freedom-seeking people
passed through William's line
of the Underground Railroad network,
led by Harriet "Moses" Tubman herself,
who had gone into the belly of the South
to rescue them.
William's committee provided them with money
and replaced their worn shoes.

William's work
grew two, three—four times as long!
His records helped reunite families,
torn apart by slavery,
to find each other once they'd found freedom.

But when enslaved people escaped,
their Southern enslavers lost money,
They demanded new laws.

In 1850, the Fugitive Slave Act was enacted.
It required the return of runaways
who had been captured,
even if they had found their way to freedom.
People living in free states,
where slavery was outlawed,
were forced to cooperate with the law,
or be brutally punished.

The Fugitive Slave Act resulted
in the kidnapping of free Black people
by greedy slave catchers
and federal agents.
No Black person,
free or not, North or South,
was safe.

William's work now put him in great danger.
His records were evidence of crimes committed.

William had a plan.
He bundled his records,
all those stories,
and placed them where no one would think to look.
In the back of a cemetery. Inside a dark vault.
Among the rats and the dead.

The laws were meant
to shut down the Underground Railroad.
But shut it down, they did not.

In Pennsylvania and New York,
Michigan and Vermont,
Black people, Black neighborhoods, Black churches
drove the Underground Railroad
full steam North,
carrying freedom-seeking people
straight on into Canada,
known as "Freedom's Land,"
where they would be safe.

William's work at the Anti-Slavery Society
was outstanding.
But after fourteen long years,
he made barely any more money
than he had on the day he started.

Helping freedom seekers was his passion.
But passion didn't put food on the table
for his growing family.
It was time for a change.

William resigned from his job
at the Anti-Slavery Society.
He started a coal business.

In 1860, the United States
was bitterly divided
over the issue of slavery.
War broke out. Many died.

In 1861, a new president was elected.
Could Abraham Lincoln reunite the country?
Would he choose freedom or slavery?
In time, Lincoln did the right thing.
He chose freedom.

William's coal business thrived
in the shadow of the Civil War.
By the 1870s, he was one
of the richest Black men of his time.

But even now,
life was still not always fair–
especially to Black people.
William used his power and influence to help.

Black children had been excluded from the YMCA.
So William helped start a branch for them.

Black people had been forbidden
from riding Philadelphia city streetcars.
So William protested–and won!

Henry Box Brown arri

his marvelous escape from slavery in a

Harriet Tubman had been their "Moses," b

She had faithfully gone down into Egypt.

Of course, Harriet was supreme, and

Ellen and William Craft w

as with thousands of others, the desire to be free was very strong. For this jewel they

Ellen being fair enough to pass for white, of necessity wo

Slavery brought about many radical changes.

In 1872, he published his book,
The Underground Rail Road,
a collection of stories
of hardship and hairbreadth escapes.

William Still's records,
and the stories he preserved,
reunited families
torn apart by slavery.

Because that's what stories can do.
Protest injustice.
Soothe. Teach. Inspire. Connect.
Stories save lives.

William's stories needed to be told,
so slavery's nightmare
will never happen again.

The Life and Times of
WILLIAM STILL

William Still is born.	**1821**	
Still moves to Philadelphia at age 23. He spends the next three years working a variety of jobs.	**1844**	
Still marries Letitia George. They have four children. Still goes to work for the Pennsylvania Society for the Abolition of Slavery.	**1847**	
	1848	Ellen and William Craft escape from slavery.
	1849	Henry "Box" Brown and Harriet Tubman escape from slavery.
Peter Still, William Still's brother, arrives in Philadelphia.	**1850**	The Fugitive Slave Act is passed by the US Congress. Harriet Tubman makes arrangements with William Still to rescue her family members from slavery.
Still begins a campaign to end racial discrimination on Philadelphia streetcars.	**1859**	
Still hides his record books and papers in the loft of the Lebanon Cemetery building.	**1860**	Abraham Lincoln is elected president.
Still leaves the Pennsylvania Society for the Abolition of Slavery and opens a coal and ice yard.	**1861**	The Civil War begins.
	1863	Abraham Lincoln issues the Emancipation Proclamation, an executive order ending slavery in the Confederate states. It does not apply to border states like West Virginia and Louisiana.
	1865	The Civil War ends. Congress passes the Thirteenth Amendment, abolishing slavery throughout the United States. The Pennsylvania state legislature passes a law prohibiting discrimination on streetcars.
	1870	The Fifteenth Amendment, granting African-American men the right to vote, is ratified.
Still publishes his first book, *The Underground Rail Road*.	**1872**	
Still organizes one of the earliest YMCAs for Black children.	**1880**	
William Still dies.	**1902**	

Source: William Still: An African American Abolitionist, *stillfamily.library.temple.edu/stillfamily/exhibits/show/ william-still/timeline/timeline--the-life-and-times-o*

AUTHOR'S NOTE

My mom has always been my biggest supporter and influence. When I was a kid, she provided art supplies, encouragement, and prayers. She still does the same today, but she also sends books—as gifts and inspiration for stories I might want to write.

Not long ago, she sent a battered copy of *The Biographical Dictionary of Black Americans* by Rachel Kranz. I didn't think much of it at the time—I mean, Mom's always sending me stuff. The book is a who's-who of Black history figures, with stories and photographs. During the following Black History Month, I decided to sketch portraits from the book, one drawing a day, and post them to my social networks. (The complete collection can be downloaded for free here: *www.dontate.com/2013/03/black-history-printables.*)

At first, I focused on familiar people like Dr. Martin Luther King Jr., Bessie Coleman, and Barack Obama. But then I decided to place more emphasis on lesser-known historical figures like Osborne Anderson, Eartha Kitt, and Angela Davis. Then one day, I came across the entry for William Still, "leader of the Underground Railroad."

My curiosity was piqued. Harriet Tubman was the only name I was familiar with regarding the Underground Railroad. I knew she had helped funnel hundreds of freedom-seeking people North to free states, and on up to Canada. But I'd never heard of William Still, or any other Black person associated with the Underground Railroad system—other than the numerous brave runaways.

At his death, William Still, a free Black resident in nineteenth-century Philadelphia, was eulogized as the "Father of the Underground Railroad." He was also a best-selling author of a book called *The Underground Rail Road.* Why his relative obscurity?

Well, a lot of it pointed back to the racism of the time. The Underground Railroad has been painted with a lopsided lens. The Underground Railroad truly united Blacks and whites in a common cause—to help the enslaved seek liberty. But after slavery ended, white abolitionists went on to tell romantic stories of the Underground Railroad, centering themselves as the heroes, and downplaying the contributions of African Americans. Thankfully, Harriet Tubman fared well with the tellers of history. Other Blacks like William Still, and so many others, not so much.

In 1898, historian Wilbur Siebert published what was probably the most extensive accounting of the Underground Railroad of his generation. For his book, *The Underground Railroad from Slavery to Freedom*, he interviewed more than twenty-five hundred people, including agents and conductors who'd worked the Underground Railroad. These were first-person accounts, but most of those people were white. Only a few hundred book-length slave narratives have been published.

Philadelphia was home to the largest population of free Blacks in the country at that time, and they played a major role in helping enslaved people escape to places in the North. They were ardent opponents to slavery, and were more likely than others to participate directly in slave rescues—like helping runaways cross rivers safely into freedom. Free Blacks were active conductors and agents in the Underground Railroad, well-connected and knowing where to send freedom seekers where they could be safe. During the years leading up to the Civil War, churches, like the African American Episcopal Church, offered lodging, food, clothing, and financial support to freedom seekers passing through.

I decided to write this book about William Still because, I felt, his story needed telling. His time was overdue. My hope is that this book will help raise awareness of his contributions to the Underground Railroad, as well as the tens of thousands of other free Black Philadelphians who worked tirelessly on behalf of their people.

I'll bet my sweet mom had no idea what she was doing when she sent me that book. Or, maybe she did.

BIBLIOGRAPHY

You can read several versions of William Still's writing

Selections from his original journals have been digitized by the Historical Society of Pennsylvania. **Journal C of the Underground Railroad 1852–1857.** *www.hsp.org/history-online/digital-history-projects/pennsylvania-abolition-society-papers/ journal-c-of-station-no-2-william-still-1852-1857-0at.*

Still used his journals as the basis for his book **The Underground Rail Road. A Record of Facts, Authentic Narratives, Letters, & C., Narrating the Hardships, Hairbreadth Escapes and Death Struggles of the Slaves in Their Efforts for Freedom,** which was published in 1872 by Porter & Coates in Philadelphia,. *www.gutenberg.org/files/15263/15263-h/15263-h.htm.*

In 1885, Still published the book himself and added autobiographical material. **Still's Underground Rail Road Records: With a Life of the Author.** *catalog.hathitrust.org/Record/009789458.*

Quotations in the text are from the following sources

6   "I will die before…"
The Underground Rail Road. A Record of Facts, Authentic Narratives, Letters, & C., Narrating the Hardships, Hairbreadth Escapes and Death Struggles of the Slaves in Their Efforts for Freedom. Philadelphia: Porter & Coates, 1872. p 37.

18   "I go for liberty…"
Still's Underground Rail Road Records: With a Life of the Author. Philadelphia: William Still Publishers, 1885. p. xviii.

William Still, 1898

Other Sources

*Bentley, Judith. **"Dear Friend" Thomas Garrett & William Still, Collaborators on the Underground Railroad.** New York: Cobblehill Books, 1997.

Blight, David W. **Passages to Freedom: The Underground Railroad in History and Memory.** Washington, DC: Smithsonian Books, 2004.

Blockson, Charles L. **The Underground Railroad in Pennsylvania.** Jacksonville, NC: Flame International, 1981. pp 8–32.

Borome, Joseph A. **"The Vigilant Committee of Philadelphia."** *Pennsylvania Magazine of History and Biography 92*, (January 1968), pp 320–351.

*Boyd, James P. **William Still: His Life and Work to This Time.** Galloway, NJ : South Jersey Culture & History Center, 2017.

Foner, Eric. **Gateway to Freedom: The Hidden History of the Underground Railroad.** New York: W. W. Norton & Company, 2016.

Gara, Larry. **"William Still and the Underground Railroad."** *Pennsylvania History: A Journal of Mid-Atlantic Studies*, Vol. 28, No. 1 (January, 1961), pp. 33–44.

*Gates, Jr. Henry Louis. **"Who Really Ran the Underground Railroad?"** *www.pbs.org/wnet/african-americans-many-rivers-to-cross/history/who-really-ran-the-underground-railroad*

*Gibson, J. W. and W. H. Crogman. **The Colored American from Slavery to Honorable Citizenship.** Atlanta: J. L. Nichols & Co., 1902. Available online at catalog.hathitrust.org/Record/009578199

*Khan, Lurey. **One Day, Levin…He Be Free: William Still and the Underground Railroad.** New York: E. P. Dutton, 1972.

*Khan, Lurey. **William Still and the Underground Railroad: Fugitive Slaves and Family Ties.** New York, iUniverse, 2010.

*Newman, Richard S. **"Abolitionism"** from **The Encyclopedia of Greater Philadelphia.** *www.philadelphiaencyclopedia.org/archive/abolitionism/#4973*

Pinsker, Matthew. **"William Still and the History of the Underground Railroad"** Paper delivered at Clarke Center Occasional Papers Series. Paper #15 (February 24, 2003).

*Siebert, Wilbur H. **The Underground Railroad from Slavery to Freedom: A Comprehensive History.** New York: Macmillan, 1989.

*Still, James. **Early Recollections and Life of Dr. James Still.** Published by the author in 1877.

*Swital, William J. **Underground Railroad in Pennsylvania.** Mechanicsburg, PA: Stackpole Books, 2001.

***"William Still: An African American Abolitionist."** Temple University Library. *stillfamily.library.temple.edu/stillfamily/exhibits/show/william-still.*

*These works were particularly helpful.

Harriet Tubman   Dec. 29/54

(6) Arrived_ John Chase, (now Dan.

Lloyd), Benj. Ross (now Jas. Stewart)

Henry Ross,(now Lewis Stewart),

Peter Jackson, (now Stanch Tilghman)

Jane Kane, (now Catherine K.)

Robert Ross

John is 20 yrs of age,

chesnut color, spair built, Smart &c

He fled from John Campbell Henry, a farmer, who

resided at Cambridge, Dorchester, Md.

John spoke of his master as being a hard

man_ owns 140 slaves. Some hes

sells, occasionally_